The use of too many questions has been avoided, as it is more important to encourage comment and discussion than to expect particular answers.

Care has been taken to retain suf[ficient] realism in the illustrations and sub[ject] matter to enable a young child to [begin] identifying objects, creatures and situations.

It is wise to remember that patienc[e and] understanding are very important, a[nd that] children do not all develop evenly or at the same rate. Parents should not be anxious if children do not give correct answers to those questions that are asked. With help, they will do so in their own time.

The brief notes at the back of this book will enable interested parents to make the fullest use of these **Ladybird talkabout** books.

Publishers: Ladybird Books Ltd . Loughborough
© Ladybird Books Ltd 1974
Printed in England

compiled by Ethel Wingfield

illustrated by Eric Winter, Harry Wingfield
and Martin Aitchison

The publishers wish to acknowledge the assistance of
the nursery school advisers who helped with the
preparation of this book,
especially that of Mrs. Nora Britton, Chairman,
and Miss M. Puddephat, M.Ed., Vice Chairman
of The British Association for Early Childhood
Education (formerly The Nursery School Association).

talkabout
the beach

Talk about the picture

Talk about the colours

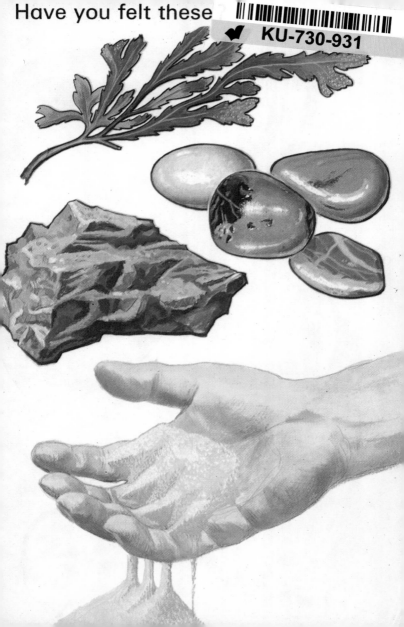

LOOK and find
another like this

and this

and this

Tell the story

1

3

Talk about the picture

What are they for ?

Tell
the story

Which live in the sea?

See what happens
to the ice-cream

Talk about the picture

Big and little

Which would you
like to take
on a picnic?

Tell the story

1

3

Talk about
the
photograph

1

2

3

4

5

Counting shells
and sand pies.

Talk about
the games

Talk about the fish
and their colours

Tell the story

Match each picture with its black sha

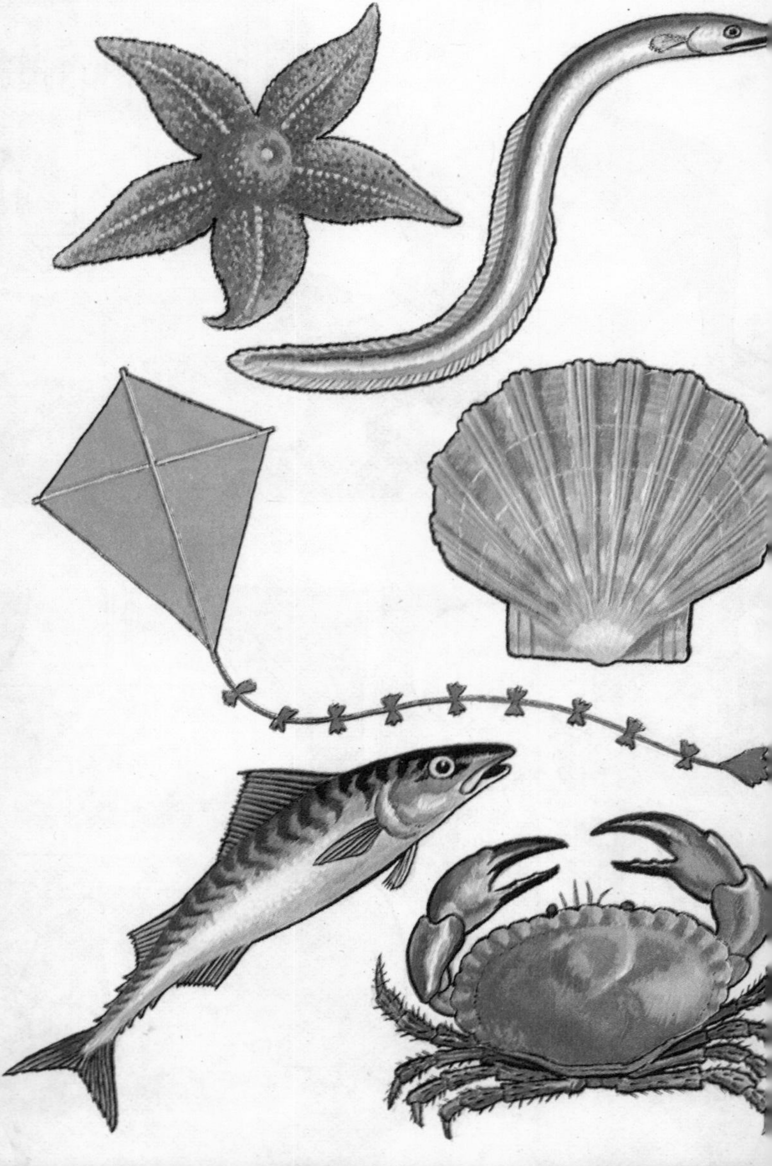

Talk about day-time and night-time

Who has caught the fish?

Talk about the picture

KEEP THE BEACH TIDY

Which sho
put in

ve been
sket ?

Suggestions for extending the use of this **talkabout** book . . .

The page headings are only brief suggestions as to how the illustrations can be used. However, these illustrations have been planned to help children understand various important concepts during their discussions with you. For example, you can talk about children being **in** the water or standing **on** the side of the swimming bath or the fish being **under** the water. You can also talk about the various human actions to be seen in the pictures – running, jumping, splashing, swimming, throwing, sliding, standing, sitting, etc., and of the human emotions – surprise, happiness, anger, dismay. All these words are essential to a child's increasing understanding and vocabulary.

In many of the illustrations (particularly, for example, the 'Look and find another like this' and 'Match each picture with its black shape') visual differences of shape and colour can be pointed out. The ability to